SIAM

An Introduction to Service Integration and Management/ Multi-Sourcing Integration for IT Service Management

SIAM/MSI

An Introduction to Service
Integration and Management/
Multi-Sourcing Integration for
IT Service Management

DAVID CLIFFORD

IT Governance Publishing

Every reasonable effort has been made to ensure that the information contained in this book is accurate at the time of going to press, and the publisher and the author cannot accept responsibility for any errors or omissions, however caused. Any opinions expressed in this book are those of the author, not the publisher. Websites identified are for reference only, not endorsement, and any website visits are at the reader's own risk. No responsibility for loss or damage occasioned to any person acting, or refraining from action, as a result of the material in this publication can be accepted by the publisher or the author.

Apart from any fair dealing for the purposes of research or private study, or criticism or review, as permitted under the Copyright, Designs and Patents Act 1988, this publication may only be reproduced, stored or transmitted, in any form, or by any means, with the prior permission in writing of the publisher or, in the case of reprographic reproduction, in accordance with the terms of licences issued by the Copyright Licensing Agency. Enquiries concerning reproduction outside those terms should be sent to the publisher at the following address:

IT Governance Publishing
IT Governance Limited
Unit 3, Clive Court
Bartholomew's Walk
Cambridgeshire Business Park
Ely
Cambridgeshire
CB7 4EA
United Kingdom

www.itgovernance.co.uk

The author has asserted the rights of the author under the Copyright, Designs and Patents Act, 1988, to be identified as the author of this work.

First published in the United Kingdom in 2016
by IT Governance Publishing.

ISBN 978-1-84928-851-4

FOREWORD

Business demand for improved delivery times, increased flexibility and improved cost efficiencies is driving organisations to engage with a broader range of specialised IT service providers. But the integration of multiple service providers can present several challenges for an organisation.

David has written an excellent pocket guide that provides deep insight into service integration and management. He clarifies the key concepts, explores various operating models and describes the key functions that are required - both operationally, as well as at a strategic level, to support of the proper governance of IT across the extended IT supply chain.

I am sure that this guide will assist business and IT professionals alike and would recommend it to all involved in crafting multiple-IT service provider strategies for their organisations.

Max Blecher, Managing Director: Virtual Alliance

Chair: JTC1/SC40 Study Group on the governance and service management of IT and IT-enabled business services provided by multiple service providers.

PREFACE

This introduction to Service Integration and Management (SIAM)/Multi-Sourcing Integration (MSI) is intended to provide an operating model overview and evidence as to why it should be used to assist with seamless IT service management (ITSM) integration of the supply chain in a multi-sourced environment.

SIAM and MSI are synonymous with each other, therefore, for the rest of this pocket guide, the term SIAM will solely be used to ease reading.

At the time of writing, there is no formal best practice guidance for the SIAM operating model. However, existing frameworks can certainly help towards the goal of seamless ITSM integration, such as ITIL®, COBIT®, e-SCM, and BISL®. Additionally, international standards are being refreshed to include references to SIAM capabilities, such as ISO/IEC 20000 (ITSM) and ISO/IEC 30105 (IT Enabled Services for Business Process Outsourcing).

This pocket guide will help you to answer a number of initial questions that you may have regarding service integration, including; What is service integration? When is SIAM applicable? What approach should be taken when sourcing ITSM services in a multi-sourced environment?

ABOUT THE AUTHOR

David Clifford is a Director at Pace Harmon, an international advisory firm headquartered in the United States of America. Pace Harmon supports clients in their most critical outsourcing, technology sourcing, service and program optimisation, and transformation programs.

David has written and contributed to a number of publications in the ITSM space, including ITIL®, service agreements and international standards. He also initiated, contributed to the development and assisted with the promotion of EXIN's ITSM qualification programme based on ISO/IEC 20000.

He is a former President of itSMF International's priSM credentialing programme that has now been superseded by the AXELOS Limited credentialing programme.

He is currently Chair of the BSI committee on IT governance (ISO/IEC 38500) and contributes to the development of the ITSM standard (ISO/IEC 20000) and BPO for the IT Enabled Services standard (ISO/IEC 30105).

He holds the O-1 visa granted by the US Government that is reserved for those who have reached the top of their field.

Email: *dclifford@paceharmon.com*

Web: *www.paceharmon.com*

Twitter: @paceharmon

ACKNOWLEDGEMENTS

The following people have generously given of their own time by reviewing this publication:

Max Blecher, Virtual Alliance, South Africa

David Bruem, Deloitte, Ireland

Rob Brus, Agrium, Canada

Alison Cartlidge, Sopra Steria, UK

John Deland, itSMF, Canada

Steven Freeman, HWC, USA

Terry Fung, AON, USA

John Gilmore, USA

Steve Keegan, Pace Harmon, USA

Cathy Kirch, itSMF, USA

Silvia Prickel, United Airlines, USA

Nathalie Rachline, Agrium, USA

Doug Read, UK

Andy Sealock, Pace Harmon, USA

Doug Tedder, Tedder Consulting, USA

Craig Wright, Pace Harmon, USA

Sun Zhenpeng, Best Practice Alliance, China

Milan Živković, itSMF, Serbia

CONTENTS

INTRODUCTION

Service Integration and Management (SIAM) is one of the latest industry buzzwords. However, SIAM is much more than a buzzword as it represents a real way of addressing the multi-sourcing challenge facing organisations today when outsourcing to many service providers to provide a holistic service to the customer organisation. The need for an approach to integrate services has been brought into stark focus by the increasing popularity of Infrastructure (IaaS), Software (SaaS) and Platform (PaaS) "as-a-Service" offerings.

Many commercial service providers are now starting to embrace the SIAM model and re-engineer their traditional managed service offerings to support the increasing demand for "SIAM-as-a-Service".

SIAM is an ITSM operating model that is focused on ensuring that the supply chain aligns with the agreed needs of the demand, i.e. the customer organisation, in a seamless and integrated manner, see Figure 1.

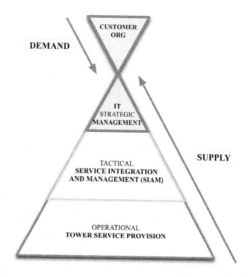

Figure 1 : Customer demand and IT supply

This pocket guide will explore the various characteristics of this IT operating model. It will also discuss the merits of a single versus multi-sourced approach when outsourcing service towers, such as data centre and managed print services.

IT organisations are realising that they need a way of integrating and aggregating service provision and performance in order to maintain their commitments to their customers. They are turning away from the traditional single-sourced managed service provision (MSP) strategy to a multi-sourced strategy due to a "best-in-class" sourcing strategy being used, which is initiated by customer demand for agility, innovation, and enhanced service provision. Quite often, this approach will include cloud-based virtualised computing resource solutions known as Infrastructure-as-a-Service and application solutions known as Software-as-a-Service.

Service integration places an emphasis on seamless interaction within the supply chain, depicted by the line between tower service providers, the service integrator, and into the retained IT organisation in Figure 2.

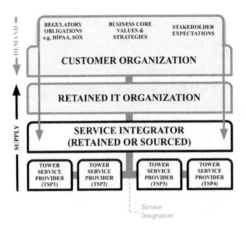

Figure 2 : Service integration alignment

NOTE: this diagram is not intended to show the contractual relationship between the service integrator and the tower service providers. In practice, there are many contractual relationship combinations that may be in use. For example, the retained IT organisation direct to the service integrator and each tower service provider plus the retained IT organisation to the service integrator who may also be providing one or more tower services. These contractual and operating models will be explored further in this pocket guide.

Finally, to ensure that the SIAM operating model can function effectively, a strategic management layer must be in place and retained somewhere within the customer organisation, typically with the retained IT function. This function will ensure that service integrator and tower service providers perform to the contractual expectations.

CHAPTER 1: TYPES OF OUTSOURCING

While a SIAM operating model provides a method of integrating and aggregating service provision and performance, it is important to understand what types of outsourcing exist that need to be integrated and managed. The three main types are:

1. IT Outsourcing (ITO)

At its core, IT Outsourcing (ITO) is nothing more than the use of third-party resources to provide IT facilities and perform IT infrastructure services historically performed by internal personnel. Typical IT infrastructure towers/services include:

- Cross-functional services (for example, ITSM processes such as change and release and deployment management).

- Service desk services.

- End user services.

- Managed print services.

- Distributed network services.

- Unified communication (collaboration) services.

- Data centre services (for example, server management, storage management, and database administration).

- Identity and access management services.

- Managed security services.

- Asset management services.

- Colocation services.

2. Application Development and Maintenance (ADM) – part of ITO

Application Development and Maintenance (ADM) addresses two core application disciplines:

1. **Development**: the design and development of tailored applications, and customisation or configuration of packaged applications, (including custom code, reports, interfaces to other systems) to address an organisation's specific business requirements.

2. **Maintenance:** Ongoing support (to resolve incidents/problems faced by business users and to perform minor enhancements) of the applications portfolio (i.e. "to keep them running").

3. Business Process Outsourcing (BPO)

Business Process Outsourcing (BPO) encompasses the outsourcing of one or more business processes to a service provider who uses technology to deliver the service, otherwise known as IT Enabled Services-Business Process Outsourcing (ITES-BPO).

Examples of business processes that may be in the scope of an outsourcing arrangement include:

- Finance
- Healthcare
- Human resource management
- Logistics

The services in the ITO, ADM and BPO arena are often grouped and referred to as "towers" within the context of IT sourcing. This term will be used throughout this pocket guide when referring to these types of services.

Outsourcing considerations

A well-executed and managed outsourcing relationship has many positive aspects, including value enhancement, cost savings and reducing non-strategic focus. Conversely, there are also potential downsides including diminished control and the loss of internal capabilities. Examples of considerations for outsourcing are listed here:

Cost reduction and value enhancement

- Cost reduction is typically achieved through the vendor's ability to use economies of scale, or to optimise the process by using pre-existing processes and toolsets.

- Cost reduction can be achieved through labour arbitrage where jobs move to countries where labour and the cost of doing business are less expensive.

- Value can also be enhanced in other ways besides cost reduction (for example, mitigation of liability and/or risk).

- The performance of the business process may be improved through the vendor's ability to incorporate best practices, rapidly deploy new technologies, or provide more specialised staff on-demand.

Enhanced IT focus on corporate strategy

- A good outsourcing relationship should require less time, effort and resources to manage than an in-house operational process. This can be achieved by simplifying management by focusing on business outcomes rather than management of the people and processes to achieve a specific result.

- Reduced time spent on operationalising non-strategic areas and building or retaining skill sets to maintain them enables retained IT resources to be applied to higher priority and more strategic tasks.

Enhanced access to skilled resources

- Rather than acquiring and maintaining hard-to-find skills, this responsibility shifts to the outsourcer.

- The outsourcer's scale allows for the flexible allocation of resources to meet peaks and troughs in demand, including the short-term assignment of specialist resources to meet transient requirements.

- Depending on the service provider's service delivery location(s), additional advantages in resource availability may also be gained from accessing qualified resources from other labour markets.

CHAPTER 2: MOVING FROM THE TRADITIONAL MSP MODEL

IT organisations have previously outsourced their service provision to a single managed service provider (MSP) or, in other words, sole-sourced. The MSP would largely focus on internal tower service provision (TSP) support, for example, service desk and collaboration services.

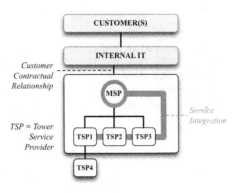

Figure 3 : Traditional MSP model

Under this model, the MSP would be accountable for all services and tower service providers that are defined within the scope of the master services agreement (MSA) between the customer organisation and the MSP.

The customer organisation relies on a single MSP to provide outsourced services for the term of the agreement, subject to normal termination clauses.

It should be noted that the MSP might sub-contract elements of service provision, as an example, see Figure 3's TSP4. This may occur because the customer has specified that the MSP must use particular service providers or because the MSP does not have the required competence or geographic presence for some towers to achieve the agreed service levels. Additionally, there may be an inherited situation where the customer organisation has a number of existing service provider contracts that they wish to retain.

The provisions of the MSA set boundaries around all of the services and may define those services that the customer deems to be important that only the MSP must perform, as opposed to subcontracting those services.

Indeed, the MSP will largely wish to retain service provision in-house in order to maximise the quality of service, minimise risk, and preserve its margins.

From a customer perspective, while it might be convenient to contract via a single-sourcing model, there can also be downsides. Rarely does one-size fit all and the provider may have capability across all of the towers, but is unlikely to be "best-in-class" for each and every tower. Also, in order to incentivise the MSP to invest in transformation and to commit to productivity gains throughout the term of the agreement, MSP contracts tend to be long-term, typically ranging from three to five years.

In today's competitive marketplace for commoditised services, organisations are looking to focus back on what differentiates them, as opposed to investing in non-core activities. Additionally, organisations are seeking:

- More agility from its commoditised service provision to enable them to change strategic direction more easily through "plug and play" and "as-a-Service" IT provision.

- Market-leading service providers who utilise intimate knowledge of how to optimise delivery of their services to increase the probability of service availability, reliability, and innovation.

Multi-sourcing supports this industry direction by providing diverse service delivery models. This places a whole new emphasis on the capability to integrate the service providers into one seamless and cohesive unit. This is a challenging role that many organisations have looked to take on board themselves through investment in their people and technical resources but, as organisations focus more heavily on their strategic core, external integration services are becoming more prevalent.

Therefore, service providers have begun to re-align their offerings to include a capability for Service Integration And Management (SIAM) to address this need, "SIAM-as-a-Service".

CHAPTER 3: SOURCING MARKET TRENDS

Service providers are increasing in number on a regular basis. OEMs (original equipment manufacturers) and COTS (commercial off the shelf) providers have been focusing beyond product supply and on providing a cloud-based product service such as Infrastructure-as-a-Service or Software-as-a-Service. These new offerings are complementing traditional tower-based services such as data centre services and unified communications, for example.

Customer organisations are taking more of a "plug and play" approach to sourcing their service providers, looking for agility, innovation, and cost reduction. This strategy is leading to an increasing prevalence of multi-sourced models.

Such multi-sourcing approaches demand an integrated approach to bring the service providers together to fulfil the holistic service provision vision of the customer organisation.

Multi-sourcing explained

The customer organisation commits to separate contracts with service providers for individual or logical bundles of towers. For example, ERP (enterprise resource planning), data centre, service desk, end user, network and accounts payable services could all form individual tower bundles.

By taking this approach, the customer organisation has a number of advantages, for example:

- There is competition between existing tower service providers for new services. For example, tower service providers "A", "B" and "C" include managed security services in their service portfolio in addition to the services already contracted for. The customer organisation may request each tower provider to bid for any new managed service. The customer is therefore capitalising on a pre-qualified market for new service bids, thereby reducing the risk of open market tendering.

Contracts can be organised so that not all contracts are in a renewal review stage at the same time. This has many benefits, the main one being that the customer organisation has mitigated the risk of the MSP single-sourcing model where all services are expiring at the same time. This gives the MSP more negotiation strength and the customer greater exposure should the relationship have broken down.

NOTE: a multi-sourced approach can still be taken should contracts expire at the same time.

- Dependent on the tower in focus, the customer has the ability to change tower service providers without necessarily affecting the other towers, unless there are clear dependencies defined.

Service integration

To ensure that the services are aligned with the overall expectations of the customer and that all of the contracted parties work together, a service integrator, fulfilling service integration activities, is required, see Figure 4.

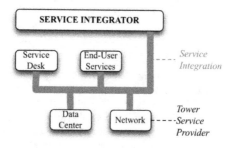

Figure 4 : Service integration

The service integrator is accountable for ensuring that all of the tower service providers perform to provide a seamless service that is aligned to the contractual commitments that have been made with the customer organisation. This differs from the traditional MSP model as most service providers are external to the service integrator organisation and, therefore, demand more stringent integration. Typical activities of the service integrator include:

- Communicate and manage alignment to customer organisation policies and standards.

- Define, review and maintain end-to-end service level agreements.

- Conduct tower service provider process audits and quality assurance reviews for adherence to contractual obligations.

- Measure and monitor process performance (effectiveness) regularly.

- Manage end-to-end service level management performance retaining overall accountability.

- Manage cross-tower corrective actions, continual service improvement and innovation activities.

- Manage cross-tower incidents and root cause analysis activities, especially major incident management.

- Manage cross-tower change and release management.

- Manage end-to-end change and release management planning.

- Provide and manage an ITSM tool to aggregate ITSM lifecycle events and information related to service performance.

Service integration is necessary to ensure that, subject to the contracted scope, the design, transition, operation and improvement activities are aligned. The procedures for each of the processes within the service management lifecycle stages must have appropriate integration points identified in order for the model to be effective. For example, defining the touch-points between the service desk tower and the network tower service provider during the course of an incident or defining how and when the service level performance will be reported by a managed print services tower to the integrator. These touch-points can be documented in operational level agreements (OLAs), sometimes known as cross-vendor procedures (CVPs). The content of these documents often includes:

- Establishing a process to address multiple tower disputes.

- Promoting a philosophy of "fix first, address later" for issues.

- Establishing a method to hold a tower service provider accountable for the confirmed service failure caused by another tower. This may be similar to a service credit regime.

- Circumventing disputes regarding confidential information by including governance procedures.

- Imposing common IT standards.

- Imposing common touch-points for service integration.

In addition to integration, the service integrator is typically accountable for aggregating service data across all tower service providers, be they external, internal or a hybrid. Tower data that is normally considered for aggregation is as follows:

- **Configuration management**; the service integrator would manage a federated architecture that utilises the configuration management databases that the tower service providers manage throughout the configuration lifecycle. It presents them as a virtual, singular configuration management system to enable an end-to-end view.

- **Incident management**; sharing of incident data as it progresses through its life is a cornerstone of the incident management process. Service towers will provide updates related to incident resolution status, details of the resolution and user contact.

- **Service performance**; service level metrics and goals at the tower level will need to be aggregated to provide overall service performance.

- **Change and release management**; sharing of forward schedules of change and release plans to assist with alignment and reduce conflict.

Challenges with multi-sourcing

One major issue faced by organisations that wish to move to a multi-sourced model is retro-fitting integration requirements into existing service contracts where they will form a part of the future operating model. There are normally three methods that can be used to address this issue:

1. **Apply a contract change**; at an advantageous time to the customer organisation, follow the contract change process to introduce the integration requirements for the existing service provider.

2. **Wait until the contract is ready for renewal or other towers are due for renewal to assist with leverage**; dependent upon how far away the renewal date is, the customer organisation will be in a stronger position to negotiate additions to the contract at renewal time with the existing service provider than they are mid-course.

3. **Include the integration requirements when transitioning out**; should the existing service provider not feature in the new operating model, the customer organisation may choose to wait until they are ready to

either transition out to another service provider at the end of the existing service provider's contract term, or at the point of early termination.

Other challenges faced when taking a multi-sourcing approach include:

- **Protecting intellectual property rights** (IPR) **and other sensitive data**; as service expectations and service data are shared with the service integrator and across the towers, there must be clear and actionable requirements built into the contracts that protect the confidential information of each entity.

- **Addressing service gaps and overlaps**; when piecing together the jigsaw of multi-sourcing agreements, gaps and overlaps may be identified. A holistic view of service provision should be mapped to assist with mitigating this issue.

- **Ensuring accountability and ownership**; when multiple service providers are involved, there can sometimes be opportunities for the service providers to sidestep what the customer expects of them, in other words, incident bouncing. This issue can be addressed through the use of good contract structure and the definition of OLAs/CVPs to include mutually agreed roles and responsibilities.

- **Maturing the retained IT organisation in the sourcing space**; successful multi-sourcing demands a high degree of maturity in terms of defining the future state operating model, the sourcing and transition strategy, the implementation of the strategy, and then the realisation of the benefits associated with the strategy. Organisations should enter into multi-sourcing with a clear roadmap and, where needed, external support to assist them with their journey.

- **Addressing differing skill set needs within the retained IT organisation**; the cultural challenge in moving away from a tactical and operational focus to a more strategic, managerial and governance-based focus should not be underestimated. A clear definition of the future state role expectations should be documented and then assessed against the talent pool within the retained IT organisation, with follow-on actions being taken to fill any shortfall in need.

- **Understanding the direct commitments made by customer organisations with "as-a-Service" providers**; an increasingly difficult challenge to overcome is that of direct customer engagement with service providers where they enter into an agreement without involving its retained IT organisation in the process but, for example, still expect the infrastructure to support increasing cloud application service demands on the network. This can partly be addressed through strict governance of IT-enabled service contracts and promotion of why it is beneficial to the customer organisation that the retained IT function is involved in sourcing decisions.

- **Collating a holistic view of finances to better understand the actual costs of IT services**; unless there is a common cost model structure across the tower service providers, pulling together the holistic view to determining total cost of ownership (TCO) can be troublesome.

- **ITSM tool integration**; all service providers have invested in tools to assist with service provision. Integration of these tools in a multi-sourced environment can be challenging. Migration of service providers to a common platform is difficult due to the investments that they have already made. However, there are service integration software solutions that facilitate integration and aggregation of data beyond point-to-point solutions.

When a customer organisation is considering a multi-sourcing approach, they should take a top-down strategy when defining their IT operating model as this will help to mitigate the challenges mentioned here. The strategy would typically be implemented over a period of time and, therefore, would require a transformational roadmap to be defined.

CHAPTER 4: DETERMINING THE GOVERNANCE AND IT OPERATING MODEL

A key tenant for customer organisations is to retain a minimum level of strategic control and overall governance of IT service provision. This will allow it to concentrate on its strategic core while determining which services in each tower will be sourced.

The international standard ISO/IEC 38500:2015 defines governance of IT as follows: "the system by which the current and future use of IT is directed and controlled". The standard provides principles, definitions, and a model for good governance of IT, to assist those at the highest level of organisations to understand and fulfil their legal, regulatory, and ethical obligations in respect of their organisation's use of IT. It is addressed primarily to the governing body. The standard is applicable for all organisations, from the smallest to the largest, regardless of purpose, design, and ownership structure.

In addition to the principles and models referred to in ISO/IEC 38500, other parts of the standard refer to implementation (38501) plus framework and model definition (38502). This family of standards is currently being expanded to address the "assessment of the governance of IT", the "governance of data" and the "governance of IT-enabled investments".

There are three key activities that the organisation's governing body must perform when governing IT, namely:

1. **Direct**; defining strategy and policies for service provision.

2. **Evaluate**; assessing proposals and plans from the service providers.

3. **Monitor**; assessing service performance and
    conformance to documented expectations.

It is important, therefore, that capabilities should always be
retained within the customer organisation to support the
governing body in performing its IT governance role and to
ensure that the end-to-end service provision remains aligned to
the needs of the business.

Retained IT governance mechanisms are quite often under-
invested in by the customer organisation during the transition
and service delivery lifecycle stages.

In a multi-sourcing IT operating model, it is imperative that the
retained IT organisation has a clearly defined mandate with
appropriate resources to enable it to perform its function. The
future state-retained IT operating model can be implemented
over a phased period of time, focusing on priority process
areas.

Key strategic processes can be aligned to the Direct, Evaluate
and Monitor activities, however, it should be noted that the
three governance activities apply to all key processes at
different points in time. IT governance should be aligned with
overall organisational governance and its requirements should
permeate through the supply chain.

Retained IT processes aligned to "Direct"

*   **Business Relationship Management**; defining the
    strategic approach to understanding the business plans
    and objectives, achieves agreement on setting up
    effective relationships between key stakeholders,
    supports business change and acts as an advocate for the
    business in IT and for IT in the business.

*   **Demand Management**; understand and influence
    business demand, trend business demand and establish
    plans to support the agreed needs.

*   **Enterprise Architecture**; includes the assessment of

strategic capabilities and changes required to the current capabilities, the description of inter-relationships between people, processes, services, data, information, technology, and the external environment.

- **Service Portfolio Management**; define and analyse new or changed services, approve new or changed services and review the service portfolio to support the ongoing alignment to the business needs to the extent warranted.

- **Financial Management**; overall policy setting including budgeting, accounting, and charging mechanisms. Control of financial asset utilisation ensures compliance with legal and regulatory obligations.

- **Information Security Management**; ensuring that the confidentiality, integrity, and availability of the customer organisation's assets, data, information, and IT services aligns with the agreed needs and legal and regulatory requirements.

- **Vendor/Supplier Management**; definition of the vendor sourcing strategy, including strategic vendor tiering and a strategy for sourcing.

Retained IT processes aligned to "Evaluate"

- **Program and Portfolio Management**; definition, implementation, and review of portfolio structure, alignment with financial management, facilitates decisions on prioritisation of resources.

- **Continual Service Improvement**; analysing current performance across processes, procedures, people, tools, and service providers to identify improvement opportunities and manage prioritised improvements throughout their lifecycle.

Retained IT processes aligned to "Monitor"

- **Service Performance Management**; monitoring of service level agreement performance, assessing continual improvement initiatives for effectiveness.

- **Contract Management**; negotiate and resolve contractual issues, manages contractual change process, ensures legal and regulatory compliance via contracts, assesses the alignment to contractual obligations, uses KPIs to monitor and challenge performance and identify improvement opportunities.

- **Financial Management**; monitors IT expenditure and alignment to IT financial targets, monitors charge/recharge and revenue/cost recovery, establishes improvement opportunities for alignment/realignment to financial policies and plans.

- **Service Acceptance Management**; formal confirmation that pre-determined acceptance criteria have been met and that the service provider organisation is ready to operate the deployed service as per the contractual commitments.

Tactical and operational processes

The retained IT organisation may decide to perform these processes; however, they are also candidates for outsourcing to a service integrator.

If outsourced, the service integrator performs many of the tactical and operational processes under delegated authority from the customer organisation's retained IT function. However, the retained IT organisation will still define policies, objectives, metrics and goals for these process areas while allowing the service integrator to perform the day-to-day management. The tactical and operational processes are namely:

Design processes

- Service catalog management,

- Service level management,

- Availability management,

- Capacity management,

- IT service continuity management,

- Information security management,

- Supplier management.

Transition processes

- Planning and support including project management,

- Service asset and configuration management,

- Change management,

- Change evaluation,

- Release and deployment management,

- Service validation and testing,

- Knowledge management.

Operation processes

- Incident management,

- Problem management,

- Access management,

- Request fulfillment,

- Event management.

Retained IT or service integrator considerations

Many factors may be considered when deciding which processes should be outsourced to a service integrator. A selection of these is explored here:

- **Current maturity of the customer organisation's IT function**; the organisation may have a low level of maturity in particular process areas where the service integrator has put investment and has a significantly more advanced maturity, resulting in improved business alignment and an emphasis on more proactive behaviour.

- **Current maturity of the customer organisation's IT tool architecture**; the organisation may have tools that are old and difficult to integrate when considering a SIAM operating model.

- **Timescales**; business drivers, legal and regulatory requirements, and mergers and acquisitions could all influence the speed at which the IT maturity and service availability needs to develop for the introduction and maintenance of services.

- **Available skill set**; the organisation may find it difficult to source and/or retain people with the appropriate skill sets in the geographic area that they are in. This could steer the organisation towards a service integrator who has the required skill set and depth of knowledge.

- **Current maturity of the service integrator organisation's IT function**; the integrator may have a low level of maturity in particular process areas although their choice may still be attractive due to pricing or other capabilities.

CHAPTER 5: TYPES OF SERVICE INTEGRATION MODELS

There are three primary types of service integration model that are prevalent in the IT industry, namely:

1. **Internal Service Integrator (ISI)**
   Where the internal IT function takes the role of service integrator across service providers.

2. **External Service Integrator (ESI)**
   Where an external service provider is solely focused on performing "SIAM-as-a-Service", i.e. they provide the integration service but do not provide any tower services.

3. **External Tower Service Integrator (ETSI)**
   Where an external service provider performs "SIAM-as-a-Service" but also delivers one or more tower services to the customer.

Internal Service Integrator (ISI)

This model has the accountability for integration and aggregation of service performance residing with the IT function of the customer organisation.

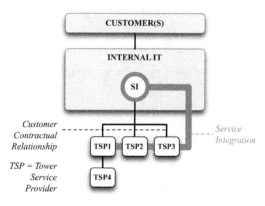

Figure 5 : Internal service integrator model

Benefits of the internal model

- The service integrator will have an intimate knowledge of the customer organisation, which helps it to understand the needs and reflect those needs in the service provision. Additionally, they will normally bring a greater degree of cultural alignment to the customer organisation.

- No complex contractual structure with an external integrator.

- High degree of transparency of service performance.

Challenges of the internal model

- Quality outcomes depend on a high degree of process and tool maturity across a wide array of ITSM processes that internal IT functions rarely have.

- The internal IT function may find it difficult to find appropriately skilled resources within the local labour market.

- Costs of retaining the required skill set are typically higher than external models.

External Service Integrator (ESI)

This model has the accountability for integration and aggregation of service performance residing with an external service integrator (ESI). The ESI has no contractual commitment to manage a tower; they are solely focused on integration and aggregation on behalf of the customer organisation.

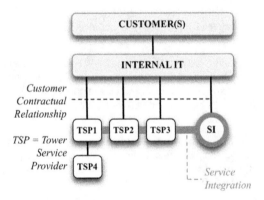

Figure 6 : External service integrator model

Benefits of the external model

- Enables the retained IT organisation to focus on strategic direction and IT governance, enabling them to focus on outcomes compared with day-to-day tactical and operational management.

- Enables the service integrator to concentrate on integration and aggregation, as opposed to also providing service delivery for other towers.

- Capitalises on the investments made by the service integrator to mature its ITSM capability including; people, process, and tools.

- The service integrator is separate from the tower service providers and, therefore, they can look at service provision with an independent perspective.

Challenges of the external model

- The service integrator does not have any direct involvement in service provision of one or more towers. This model can, therefore, be less interesting commercially for the integrator unless they look to introduce a high "integration fee" margin.

- It is more difficult for the service integrator to understand the challenges of the tower service providers if they do not provide one or more towers themselves. This can be mitigated by ensuring that the service integrator has past experience of managing such towers.

- There is a risk of activities falling into a gap with unclear accountabilities for resolution. This can be overcome through clear definition of roles and responsibilities using OLAs/CVPs.

External Tower Service Integrator (ETSI)

This model has the accountability for integration and aggregation of service performance residing with an external service provider. The service integrator is also providing one or more tower services.

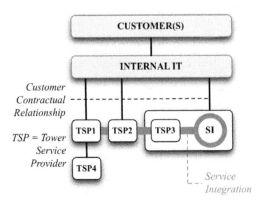

Figure 7 : External tower service integrator model

Benefits of the external integrator/tower model

- Enables the retained IT organisation to focus on strategic direction and IT governance.

- Capitalises on the investments made by the service integrator to mature its ITSM capability including; people, process, and tools.

- Ensures that the service integrator has empathy with other tower service providers.

- Provides additional revenue opportunity for the service integrator and is, therefore, more commercially interesting.

Challenges of the external integrator/tower model

- Unless the number of towers that the service integrator provides is limited to a low number, the model will be nearer to the managed services provider (MSP) model and inherent challenges that were explored earlier.

- The service integrator has the ability to manipulate the performance data of the service towers that it operates. This is why the most popular SIAM ETSI model is to source the service integration capability together with the service desk as these two disciplines cut across all of the service towers without providing a technical tower service.

CHAPTER 6: AGGREGATING SERVICE LEVEL PERFORMANCE

The service integrator should assess the performance of the tower service providers against customer organisation defined service level agreements (SLAs), promote a common understanding of SLAs throughout the supply chain, and recommend continual improvements to processes and methodologies to enable the service to continue to meet future business requirements.

The service integrator should provide the following service performance management activities:

- As each tower service provider will have its own methods of collecting and reporting on service performance, the service integrator will need to specify a common integration capability.

- Work with the tower service providers to audit data that is being used to report performance, and influence service performance improvement actions.

- Stay up-to-date on customer organisation strategies and act as a trusted advisor suggesting how industry trends may improve the service delivery and performance.

- Propose changes to SLAs to ensure that they properly reflect business needs while balancing costs.

- Proactively analyse opportunities to improve performance levels.

- Proactively troubleshoot performance issues and resolve problems that span across tower service providers.

- Identify opportunities for innovation and discuss them with the retained IT organisation during governance meetings.

- Consolidate opportunities for improvement and innovation from service tower providers and coordinate impact assessments to deliver on these opportunities.

CHAPTER 7: MULTI-SOURCING RFP APPROACH

The quality of an organisation's procurement activities directly affects its profitability and operational flexibility. If the activities are suboptimal, issues can arise, for example:

- Service contracts can tie the organisation into a long-term agreement that is not fit for purpose.

- Service overlaps can exist where the organisation is paying more than once for the services.

- Service gaps can exist and, once identified, these can be expensive to address in the time required.

- Service costs can be greater than current service provision due to poorly structured cost models.

Based on the requirements of the customer organisation, each sourcing event must appropriately balance timeliness, cost, organisational readiness, and contractual flexibility.

To enhance the degree of success in a multi-sourced environment, it is recommended that careful upfront preparation in advance of initiating the full RFP (request for proposal) process is required and should focus on addressing potential pitfalls such as incident bouncing and lack of collaboration between vendors.

RFP structure

- Common terms and agreement format for all tower service providers and the service integrator.

- Identification of services that are both in scope and out of scope.

- Common definitions and metrics, service performance targets, and service penalty/credit regimes (for example, Severity 1, Severity 2, Severity 3).

- Adoption of ITIL® (or another framework) terminology and industry-established terminology (e.g. incident versus service request versus problem).

- Common compensation structures and invoicing requirements.

- IPR (intellectual property rights) for all customer organisation data to be retained by the customer organisation.

- Adherence/conformance to standard policies/strategies, for example, security and enterprise architecture.

- Commitment to collaboration and SIAM model by agreement to CVPs.

Operational requirements

- Centralised ITSM tooling with mandated integration and aggregation.

- Common ITSM processes.

- Customer organisation determines the "systems of record" (e.g., for SLA measures).

- Tight coordination between the service desk and other vendors (for example, incident management, request fulfillment, and major incident management).

- Clear knowledge management obligations for all vendors and tracking of knowledge efficacy.

- Common configuration discovery and mapping obligations.

IT governance mechanisms

- Multi-vendor management meetings (i.e. a service management integration group) typically led by the ITSM Office (ITSMO).

- Emphasis on problem management performance and problem resolution trends to reduce service outages and associated costs.

- OLAs/CVPs approved by the customer organisation that set clear expectations for integration, service improvement and innovation (for example, to facilitate confidential data exchange, issue resolution, arbitration and so on).

During the sourcing process, there are a number of other considerations that will go into the process:

- Alignment of the tower service provider portfolio with the business objectives of the organisation, addressing critical issues such as application and asset rationalisation, the degree of consolidation, outsource versus in-source delivery, shared (cloud) versus dedicated services, and on- versus off-shore.

- Ensure that the selection, implementation, and integration of new technologies takes into account the impact to both upstream and downstream applications and related infrastructure.

- Identify vendors with delivery strengths and cultures that complement those of the customer organisation.

- Pinpoint and support the organisational and operational changes necessary to migrate to new technologies and tower service providers.

- Achieve optimal results through the negotiation process, committing the tower service provider to specific performance while also allowing the provider sufficient flexibility to apply its expertise and best practices.

- Establish and/or optimise the tower service provider management function to maximise service provider performance and extract greater ongoing value from the negotiated agreement.

All of these requirements will ultimately feed into the contractual agreement between the retained IT organisation, the service integrator, and tower service providers.

CHAPTER 8: TRANSITION STAGE

Following completion of the successful RFP stage and formal contract signature, the focus will turn to the transition of in scope responsibilities to the tower service providers and, where applicable, to the service integrator should the sourcing decision be made to outsource service integration capabilities to a "SIAM-as-a-Service" provider.

The contract resulting from the RFP stage will specify requirements and expectations of the outsourced towers. These will need to be translated into a detailed transition plan for all activities leading up to the formal service commencement date(s). Typically, the service provider develops the transition plan with oversight by the customer organisation's retained IT function.

It should be noted that the retained IT function would need to develop an over-arching transition plan for the following reasons:

- Where multiple suppliers are involved and the retained IT function is performing the role of the service integrator, for example:

    o to manage cross-tower dependencies,

    o to revise processes to align to the activities required to perform the role of the service integrator,

    o to revise the tool architecture to allow for integration and aggregation of service data and information.

- The retained IT organisation has internal transformational activities to carry out, for example:

    o cultural change activities related to moving from an operational to more strategic management focus,

- o revised processes for engagement with the core customer organisation business units,

- o revised processes for engagement with the service tower providers,

- o knowledge transfer to the service provider(s),

- o providing access to customer applications and infrastructure based on customer organisation security policies.

- The retained IT function has responsibility to provide direction, data and approvals of service provider deliverables.

Following on from the detailed planning stage, activities to support knowledge transfer and progression towards service commencement with the service provider will begin. In parallel, the customer organisation's retained IT function will progress the transformational activities.

One of the biggest challenges that customer organisations face when outsourcing is achieving a balance of continuing to perform business as usual activities, while performing transition processes to introduce a new operating model due to the additional demands on individuals' time. Examples of ways of mitigating this risk are:

- Leveraging accelerators from the chosen service providers, for example, pre-existing standard operating procedures and transition plans.

- Developing detailed transition plans that clearly call out the level of effort required by the customer organisation's staff to support the transition programme.

- Ensuring key stakeholders are included in the planning process to promote buy-in and understanding of the transition process.

- Augmenting with contractors to perform backfill activities of in-house staff involved in the transition.

- Seeking additional external consultancy support to guide the customer organisation through the outsourcing process.

After successful completion of the transition and transformation activities, the operational governance model agreed during the transition stage will come in to effect.

At this point, the benefit realisation specified in the original outsourcing business case will need to be tracked and reported to the senior customer organisation leadership team.

CHAPTER 9: LOOKING FURTHER INTO THE FUTURE

One should consider the maturity of "SIAM-as-a-Service". Service providers headquartered in Europe have tended to be more mature in their service offerings in this space. However, North American headquartered companies are rapidly catching up and investing heavily in this service.

Service providers will accelerate the definition of their multi-sourcing integration offerings under the "SIAM-as-a-Service" portfolio. These will be much more visible in marketing campaigns. The services will be more than a simple re-badging of their cross-functional process offerings.

International standards will more explicitly embrace the concepts of service integration. Indeed, the draft version of the next edition of ISO/IEC 20000 includes references to this in a new section currently titled "Integration of the service management system and the services". Also, a new standards series, ISO/IEC 30105, is in the process of publication that is focused on providing requirements and guidance for IT Enabled Services-Business Process Outsourcing.

As more organisations embrace the SIAM operating model approach to multi-sourcing, they will see improvements in service performance and have greater agility within their strategic operating model.

ADM	**Application Development and Maintenance** The process of managing the lifecycle stages of applications, e.g. from design through coding, testing and operational support/enhancements.
ANSI	**American National Standards Institute** National standards body of the USA that defines standards that are used internationally
BISL®	**Business Information Services Library** A vendor independent public domain library for the implementation of business information management
BPO	**Business Process Outsourcing** The process of finding an appropriate external business partner that can provide services in specific business areas, such as finance and logistics.
BSI	**British Standards Institute** National standards body of the UK that defines standards that are used internationally
COBIT®	**Control Objectives for Information and related Technology** A set of best practices (framework) for information technology (IT) management

COTS	**Commercial Off-The-Shelf**
	An application that is commercially available to meet a specific business or IT need.
CVP	**Cross-Vendor Procedures**
	Formal agreement between tower service providers for integration
eSCM-SP	**eSourcing Capability Model for Service Providers**
	A best practice capability model focused on; giving guidance to service providers on improving their capabilities across the sourcing lifecycle and providing customers with the opportunity to evaluate the capability of the service providers
ESI	**External Service Integrator**
	A commercial service provider that offers services to integrate multiple service providers on behalf of the customer organisation
ETSI	**External Tower Service Integrator**
	A commercial service provider that offers services to integrate multiple service providers on behalf of the customer organisation while also providing one or more tower services
IEC	**International Electrotechnical Commission**
	Prepares and publishes international standards for all electrical, electronic and

	related technologies
IPR	**Intellectual Property Rights** The legal right to specific data/information typically in the form of patents, copyrights and trademarks.
ISI	**Internal Service Integrator** The IT function of the customer organisation that provides a service to integrate multiple service providers on behalf of the customer
ISO	**International Organization for Standardisation** Global standard setting body comprised of representatives from various national standards organisations such as ANSI and BSI
ITIL®	**Information Technology Infrastructure Library** A set of practices for IT service management that focuses on aligning IT services with the needs of the customer organisation
ITO	**Information Technology Outsourcing** The engagement of commercial partners to provide IT services to the customer organisation.
ITSMF	**Information Technology Service Management Forum** A not-for-profit member-based organisation

	that promotes best practices in the ITSM field with national chapters across the globe
MSA	**Master Services Agreement** Specifies generic terms such as payment terms, product/service warranties, intellectual property ownership, dispute resolution
MSI	**Multi-Sourcing Integration** The practice of aligning management practices across service providers at key touchpoints to provide a holistic service to the end customer. Synonym of SIAM
OEM	**Original Equipment Manufacturer** An organisation that builds a specific product for use by another organisation.
OLA	**Operational Level Agreement** A formal agreement between parties to interact within specific guidelines and measurements.
RFP	**Request For Proposal** A formal document set that is used by an organisation to request business proposals from potential partners.
SIAM	**Service Integration and Management** The practice of aligning management practices across service providers at key touchpoints to provide a holistic service to the end customer. Synonym of MSI

TSP	**Tower Service Provider**
	A service provider that offers services related to specific IT capabilities that may be technical infrastructure, application or business process related

CPSIA information can be obtained
at www.ICGtesting.com
Printed in the USA
FFHW011917030219
50352355-55464FF

9 781849 288514